THE SMARTEST
DINOSAURS

BY **"DINO" DON LESSEM**
ILLUSTRATIONS BY **JOHN BINDON**

⌐ LERNER PUBLICATIONS COMPANY / MINNEAPOLIS

To Emily Lessem, my favorite niece

This book is available in two editions:
Library binding by Lerner Publications Company,
    a division of Lerner Publishing Group
Soft cover by First Avenue Editions,
    an imprint of Lerner Publishing Group
241 First Avenue North
Minneapolis, MN 55401 U.S.A.

Website address: www.lernerbooks.com

Library of Congress Cataloging-in-Publication-Data

Lessem, Don.
    The smartest dinosaurs / by Don Lessem ; illustrations by John Bindon.
        p.   cm. — (Meet the dinosaurs)
    Includes index.
    ISBN: 0-8225-1373-0 (lib. bdg. : alk. paper)
    ISBN: 0-8225-2618-2 (pbk. : alk. paper)
        1. Dinosaurs—Juvenile literature.   I. Bindon, John, ill. II. Title. III.
Series: Lessem, Don. Meet the dinosaurs.
    QE861.5.L477 2005
    567.9—dc22   2004011152

Manufactured in the United States of America
1 2 3 4 5 6 - DP - 10 09 08 07 06 05

TABLE OF CONTENTS

SMARTEST DINOSAURS

WELCOME, DINOSAUR FANS!

I'm "Dino" Don. I LOVE dinosaurs. I especially love the smart ones that remind us how special dinosaurs were. Dinosaurs were the smartest animals of their time. Here are some fast facts on the smartest dinosaurs that you'll meet in this book. Have fun!

DEINONYCHUS (dy-NAWN-ih-kuhs)
Length: 12 feet
Home: western North America
Time: 115 million years ago

GALLIMIMUS (GAL-ih-MY-muhs)
Length: 17 feet
Home: central Asia
Time: 70 million years ago

GIGANOTOSAURUS (JIHG-uh-NOH-tuh-SAWR-uhs)
Length: 45 feet
Home: southern South America
Time: 100 million years ago

LEAELLYNASAURA (lee-EHL-ihn-uh-SAWR-uh)
Length: 6 feet
Home: Australia
Time: 110 million years ago

MICRORAPTOR (MY-kroh-RAP-tohr)
Length: 1.8 feet
Home: Asia
Time: 124 million years ago

TROODON (TROH-uh-dahn)
Length: 6 feet
Home: western North America
Time: 76 million years ago

TYRANNOSAURUS REX (tih-RAN-uh-SAWR-uhs REKS)
Length: 40 feet
Home: western North America
Time: 65 million years ago
Nickname: *T. rex*

HOW SMART WERE DINOSAURS?

The sun is going down over a forest in western North America. It is 76 million years ago. In the dim light, two young *Troodon* dinosaurs are scraping at a hole in the ground. With nimble hands, they dig quickly.

They take turns digging deep into the hole.
A mousy creature darts out. With sharp
eyesight and fast fingers, one *Troodon* nabs
it. The small animal is dinner for these
smart dinosaurs.

THE TIME OF THE SMARTEST DINOSAURS

Microraptor

Deinonychus

Leaellynasaura

124 million
years ago

115 million
years ago

110 million
years ago

Troodon and other dinosaurs lived on land
millions of years ago. They were related
to reptiles, such as lizards, alligators, and
turtles. Like reptiles, dinosaurs laid eggs.
But dinosaurs were not reptiles.

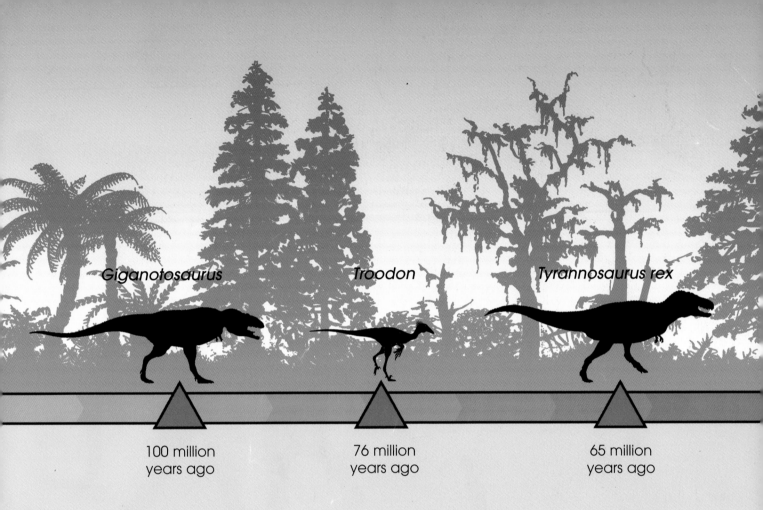

Giganotosaurus

Troodon

Tyrannosaurus rex

100 million
years ago

76 million
years ago

65 million
years ago

Dinosaurs were their own special group.

Most dinosaurs were a lot larger than reptiles.

Scientists think dinosaurs were smarter too.

But dinosaurs died out, or became **extinct,**

65 million years ago. Reptiles are still alive.

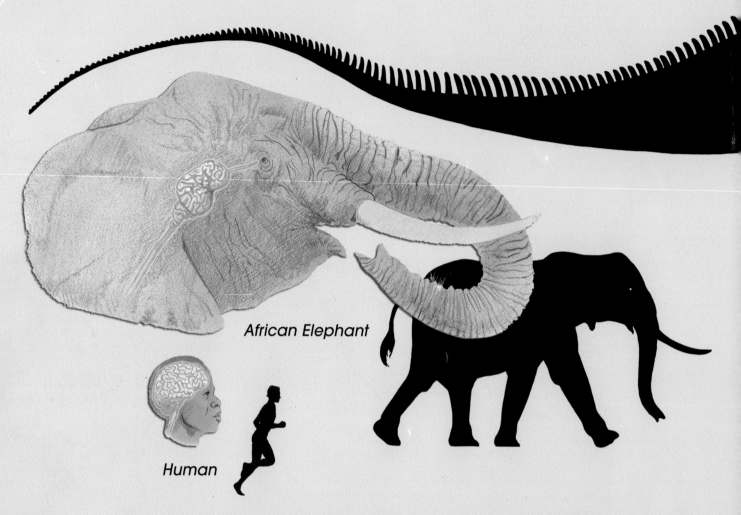

African Elephant

Human

How do we know that some dinosaurs were smarter than other animals? We can only guess. To guess how smart an animal is, scientists compare the size of its brain to the size of its body.

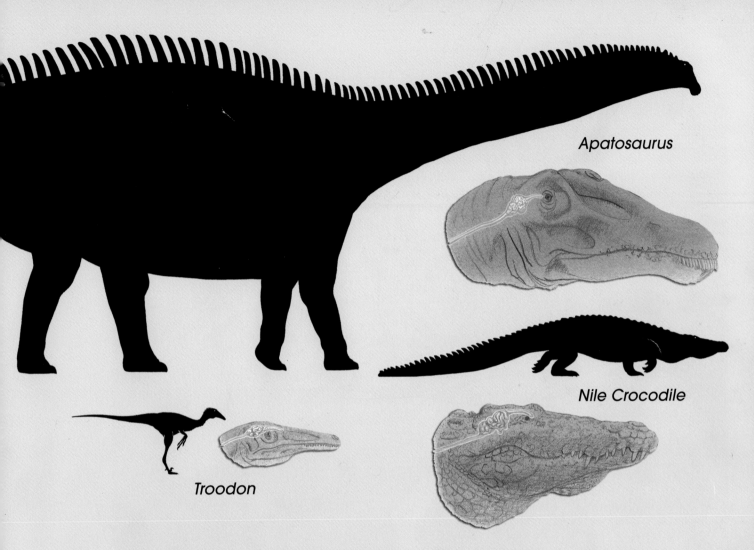

Apatosaurus

Nile Crocodile

Troodon

Humans have large brains. Elephants have
even larger brains. But this doesn't mean
that elephants are smarter than we are.
Elephants have big brains in big bodies.
We have big brains in smaller bodies.
So humans are smarter than elephants.

How do scientists know how big a dinosaur's brain was? They study the **fossils,** or remains, that dinosaurs left behind. Fossils can be bones, teeth, eggs, and even dinosaur poop.

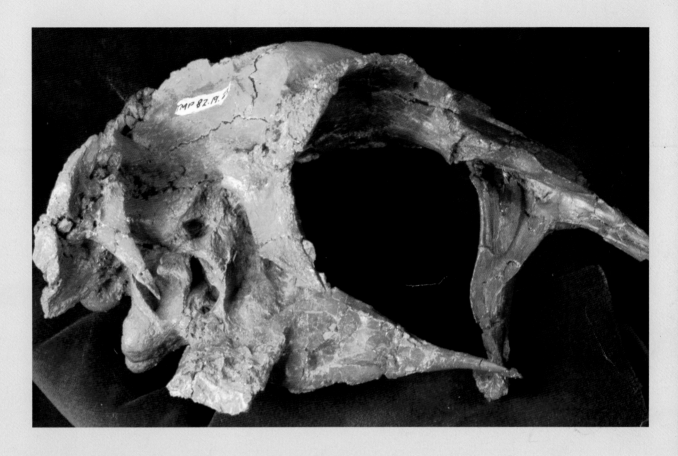

Soft body parts, such as brains, do not turn
into fossils. But sometimes a fossil of a
dinosaur's **skull** is found. Inside may be the
bony **braincase.** The braincase is the part
of the skull that holds the brain. The shape
of the braincase shows how large the
dinosaur's brain was.

DINOSAUR FOSSIL FINDS

The numbers on the map on page 15 show some of the places where people have found fossils of the dinosaurs in this book. You can match each number on the map to the name and picture of the dinosaurs on this page.

1. Deinonychus   2. Gallimimus   3. Giganotosaurus   4. Leaellynasaura

5. Microraptor   6. Troodon   7. Tyrannosaurus rex

We find dinosaur fossils all over the world. But dinosaur skulls and braincases are rarely found. In 1987, a fossil hunter made an exciting discovery in western Canada. He found the braincase of a *Troodon.*

Troodon was a little meat-eating dinosaur no bigger than a large poodle. Its big braincase proved that it had a large brain. In fact, *Troodon* is the smartest dinosaur we know of.

BIG BRAINS

Tyrannosaurus rex was one of the smartest and deadliest dinosaurs. It had a bigger brain than ours. *T. rex* also had a huge body, so it wasn't as smart as we are. But it was probably smarter than the animals it hunted.

T. rex most likely used its big brain to help it sniff food or spot **prey**, the animals it killed and ate. These two *T. rex* have teamed up to kill a duck-billed dinosaur. But they will probably end up fighting each other for the food.

Little *Leaellynasaura* are searching for food in the dim light. It is dark much of the year where they live, near Antarctica. But with their big, sharp eyes, these plant eaters can find food even in winter darkness.

Dinosaurs could see much better than many other animals. In *Leaellynasaura,* the part of the brain that helps the eyes see was very big. Seeing better helped *Leaellynasaura* live through the dark winter.

A *Giganotosaurus* roams the forests of South America. It senses the odor of rotting meat. The body of a huge dead dinosaur lies by a stream. It would smell terrible to us. But the meat smells good to this hungry *Giganotosaurus*.

Giganotosaurus could recognize many smells. A large area of its brain was used for smelling. *Giganotosaurus* could sniff out other dinosaurs, living or dead, from far away.

It is early morning in a hot desert in Asia 70 million years ago. *Tarbosaurus,* a close cousin of *T. rex,* attacks a pack of ostrichlike dinosaurs. But these scared *Gallimimus* run fast. They soon leave the tired *Tarbosaurus* far behind.

Gallimimus was one of the fastest dinosaurs. It had a light body and long legs. But running takes more than legs. Brainpower is needed to control how legs move. The large brain of *Gallimimus* helped it run.

A pack of swift *Deinonychus* is hunting.
These killers are known for their sharp
claws. They surprise a large plant eater.
It fights back, slapping members of the
pack so hard that it kills some of them.
But the hunters slash, kick, swipe, and
bite until they finally win.

Killers like *Deinonychus* and *Velociraptor*
were among the smartest of all dinosaurs.
They might have worked together to sneak
up on and surround their prey. That kind of
teamwork takes brainpower.

A young *Troodon* practices its hunting skills by chasing a moth. The moth flutters just over its head. *Troodon* tries to guess where it will dart next. SNAP! At last, the patient dinosaur succeeds.

To catch food, dinosaurs had to make their
claws move as quickly as their jaws.
Troodon could grip animals with its fingers
the same way we grab things with our thumb
and fingers. It takes a big brain to do that!

WHICH DINOSAURS WERE THE SMARTEST?

A strange little dinosaur is on the run from a much bigger dinosaur. The tiny dinosaur heads down a hill. Suddenly, it spreads its arms and takes off into the air, gliding to safety.

This little dinosaur is named *Microraptor*. It
had feathers on each of its four limbs. We
don't know for sure that *Microraptor* flew.
But it could have used its big brain to help
it move quickly. *Microraptor* might have
been the smartest dinosaur of all.

How smart would dinosaurs be if they hadn't died out? One scientist imagined they would be like humans. He created this sculpture of a supersmart animal called a dinosauroid. But dinosaurs and humans are not closely related. Few scientists think dinosaurs would look so humanlike.

The smartest dinosaurs may still be living.
Birds are close relatives of meat-eating
dinosaurs. An ostrich is about as smart as
the smartest dinosaurs. Its brain is big
compared to its body. So when you
imagine how smart the smartest dinosaurs
were, think of ostriches.

GLOSSARY

braincase: the part of the skull that holds the brain

extinct (eks-TINKT): when no members of a kind of animal or plant are living

fossils (FAH-suhlz): the remains, tracks, or traces of something that lived a long time ago

prey (PRAY): animals that other animals hunt and eat

skull: the bony part of the head

INDEX